SONIA ALLISON'S BISCUIT BOOK

GW00578079

SONIA ALLISON'S BISCUIT BOOK

PIATKUS

© 1981 Sonia Allison

First published in 1981 by Judy Piatkus (Publishers) Limited
of Loughton, Essex
Reprinted in 1982

British Library Cataloguing in Publication Data

Allison, Sonia
  Sonia Allison's biscuit book
  1. Cookies
  I. Title
  641.8'654   TX772

  ISBN 0-86188-126-5

Cover designed by Ken Leeder

Typeset by V & M Graphics Ltd., Aylesbury, Bucks
Printed and bound by R. J. Acford Ltd., Chichester

CONTENTS

INTRODUCTION

Biscuits come in many shapes, sizes, flavours and textures. They can be plain or fancy, rich or basic, crisp or soft, light or dark, and either left as they are or dolled up in fancy dress for children's parties or elegant buffets with adult overtones. Think about it. Home isn't home without the everlasting tin of biscuits; no traditional tea-table complete without the digestives, the macaroons, the coconut pyramids and melting moments; no Christmas quite the same without some crunchy, buttery shortbreads safely stored away in a kitchen cupboard; no cocktail party worthy of its name without a bowl of cheese straws or cheese biscuit butterflies on hand to pass round.

Biscuit-making forms the basis of hobby cooking, totally different from the routine and bother of family meals and therefore completely relaxing and rarely tedious. Simple biscuits are something the whole family can participate in making, while the more complicated varieties are, perhaps, best made when you have a quiet moment to yourself.

The nice thing about making biscuits is that they have a wonderful habit of working out every time. And, best of all, biscuits fresh from the oven fill the air with that happy, warm and nostalgic smell of good, old-fashioned home-baking.

TIPS

1. Do not alter the quantities given in the recipes or substitute different fats or sugars for the ones recommended.

2. Keep to the oven temperature stated. In general, you will do *less* harm if you reduce, rather than increase, the temperature.

3. Use a mixing bowl that is large enough to take all the ingredients and still enable you to work freely without the ingredients flying out over the top.

4. Place the biscuits on a shallow baking tray; a deep tray shields the biscuits round the edges from even heat.

5. Most biscuits should be left on the trays for 2 to 3 minutes before being transferred to a wire cooling rack.

6. Biscuits should be left until they are completely cold before being stored in an airtight container. If not, they will soften.

7. Cakes and biscuits should *never* be stored in the same container. If put together, the biscuits will soften.

8. Where necessary, individual hints and tips are included within the recipes.

ROLLED BISCUITS

FRUIT'N'NUT OATCAKES (Makes 16)

These not-too-sweet biscuits team very well with cheese at the end of a meal, or make an unusual mid-morning snack.

3 oz (75 g) brown flour
½ level teaspoon salt
½ level teaspoon baking powder
2 oz (50 g) butter or block margarine
5 oz (125 g) medium oatmeal
1 oz (25 g) dates <u>or</u> stoned prunes, finely chopped
1 oz (25 g) walnuts, finely chopped
1 Grade 4 (small) egg, beaten
Cold water to mix, if necessary

1. Sift the flour, salt and baking powder into a bowl. Rub in the butter or margarine until the mixture is finely blended.

2. Add the oatmeal, dates or prunes and the nuts. Mix the ingredients well together.

3. Mix to a stiff dough with beaten egg and water if necessary.

4. Turn on to a floured surface. Knead lightly until smooth.

5. Roll out fairly thinly and cut into 16 rounds with a 2-inch (5-cm) biscuit cutter.

6. Transfer to greased baking trays. Bake until lightly browned, allowing about 25 minutes in an oven preheated to 350°F/180°C, Gas Mark 4.

7. Cool on a wire rack. Store in an airtight tin when cold.

PLAIN BISCUITS

(Makes 24)

In this recipe the biscuits have all been cut into rounds, but there is nothing to stop you from using any shape of cutter you fancy to suit the occasion. From one basic recipe, you can make endless variations and produce an assortment of biscuits to please everybody.

8 oz (225 g) plain flour
½ level teaspoon salt
4 oz (125 g) butter or margarine
4 oz (125 g) caster sugar
1 teaspoon vanilla essence
3 to 4 tablespoons beaten egg

1. Sift the flour and salt into a bowl. Rub in the butter or margarine until the mixture resembles fine breadcrumbs.

2. Add the sugar. Mix to a stiff paste with essence and beaten egg, using a fork to draw the mixture together.

3. Turn on to a floured surface. Knead lightly until smooth.

4. Wrap in foil or cling film. Refrigerate for 30 minutes.

5. Roll out thinly and cut into 24 rounds, re-rolling and re-cutting trimmings to give the required number.

6. Transfer to lightly greased baking trays and bake for 12 to 15 minutes in an oven preheated to 350°F/180°C, Gas Mark 4. When ready, the biscuits should be light gold colour.

7. Transfer to a wire rack to cool. Store in an airtight tin when cold.

Cinnamon Biscuits (Makes 24)

Make as Plain Biscuits, sifting 2 level teaspoons cinnamon with the flour and salt.

Lemon Biscuits (Makes 24)

Make as Plain Biscuits, adding 2 level teaspoons finely grated lemon peel with the sugar.

Orange Biscuits (Makes 24)

Make as Plain Biscuits, adding 2 level teaspoons finely grated orange peel with the sugar.

Almond Biscuits (Makes 30)

Make as Plain Biscuits, adding 2 oz (50 g) ground almonds with the sugar. Substitute almond essence for vanilla.

Currant Biscuits (Makes 24)

Make as Plain Biscuits, adding 2 oz (50 g) currants with the sugar.

Coconut Biscuits (Makes 24)

Make as Plain Biscuits, adding 2 oz (50 g) desiccated coconut with the sugar.

Chocolate Biscuits (Makes 24)

Make as Plain Biscuits, substituting 1 oz (25 g) cocoa powder for 1 oz (25 g) flour. Use soft brown sugar instead of caster.

Ginger Biscuits (Makes 24)

Make as Plain Biscuits, sifting 2 level teaspoons powdered ginger with the flour and salt. Use soft brown sugar instead of white and omit the vanilla essence.

Coffee Biscuits (Makes 24)

Make as Plain Biscuits, sifting 1 level tablespoon instant coffee powder with the flour and salt. Omit the vanilla essence.

MADEIRA FINGERS (Makes 36)

These are elegant, old-world style biscuits which can be served for afternoon tea or used to accompany desserts.

6 oz (175 g) plain flour
Pinch of salt
4 oz (125 g) butter
3 oz (75 g) caster sugar
2 to 3 tablespoons Madeira

Topping
Beaten egg
Caster sugar

1. Sift the flour and salt into a bowl. Rub in the butter until the mixture resembles fine breadcrumbs.

2. Add the sugar. Mix to a stiff paste with the Madeira, using a fork to draw the mixture together.

3. Wrap in foil or cling film and refrigerate for 30 minutes.

4. Turn on to a floured surface and knead lightly until smooth. Roll out thinly and prick all over with the prongs of a fork.

5. Cut into approximately 36 fingers measuring 2½ x 1 inch (6.25 x 2.5 cm).

6. Transfer to lightly greased baking trays. Brush with beaten egg and sprinkle each finger with a little sugar.

7. Bake for about 15 minutes in an oven preheated to 375°F/ 190°C, Gas Mark 5. When ready, the biscuits should be a light gold colour.

8. Cool on a wire rack. Store in an airtight tin when cold.

DIGESTIVE BISCUITS (Makes 12)

Traditional mid-morning biscuits, digestives are also delicious buttered and served with cheese. For Chocolate Digestives, brush the undersides of the biscuits with melted plain or milk chocolate.

3 oz (75 g) wholemeal flour
½ oz (15 g) plain flour
½ level teaspoon baking powder
½ oz (15 g) oatmeal
1½ oz (40 g) butter
1½ oz (40 g) soft brown sugar
3 tablespoons cold milk

1. Sift the flours and baking powder into a bowl. Add the oatmeal.

2. Rub in the butter. Add the sugar. Run the mixture through the fingers to mix well.

3. Using a fork, stir in the milk to form a stiff paste.

4. Turn on to a floured surface. Knead lightly until smooth. Roll out thinly.

5. Cut into 12 rounds with a 2½-inch (6.25-cm) biscuit cutter, re-rolling and re-cutting trimmings to make the required number.

6. Transfer to greased baking trays and prick all over with a fork.

7. Bake until pale gold, allowing 15 to 18 minutes in an oven preheated to 375°F/190°C, Gas Mark 5.

8. Cool on a wire rack. Store in an airtight tin when cold.

GINGER SNAPS

(Makes 20)

Very popular with all age-groups, these crisp and buttery ginger snaps are especially designed for dunking—and the lunch box!

4 oz (125 g) self-raising flour
1 level teaspoon ground ginger
¼ level teaspoon mixed spice
2 oz (50 g) butter
1½ oz (40 g) soft brown sugar
   (light variety)
1 level tablespoon black treacle,
   melted
4 teaspoons cold milk

1. Sift the flour, ginger and spice into a bowl.

2. Rub in the butter finely. Add the sugar.

3. Mix to a stiff paste with melted treacle and milk.

4. Turn out on to a floured surface. Knead lightly until smooth.

5. Roll out as thinly as possible and cut into 20 2-inch (5-cm) rounds, re-rolling and re-cutting trimmings to make the required number of biscuits.

6. Transfer to greased baking trays. Bake for 10 minutes in an oven preheated to 350°F/180°C, Gas Mark 4.

7. Cool on a wire rack. Store in an airtight tin when cold.

SHREWSBURY BISCUITS (Makes 5)

Old-fashioned, but still worth making for the afternoon tea-table.

8 oz (225 g) plain flour
4 oz (125 g) butter or margarine
4 oz (125 g) caster sugar
Finely grated peel of 1 washed and dried small lemon
1 Grade 4 (small) egg, well beaten
6 to 7 teaspoons cold milk

Topping
Caster sugar

1. Sift the flour into a bowl. Rub in the butter or margarine. Mix in the sugar and lemon peel.

2. Using a fork, mix in the milk to form a fairly stiff dough.

3. Turn on to a floured surface and knead lightly until smooth.

4. Roll out thinly and, to keep to the traditional style, cut into 5 5-inch (12.5-cm) rounds, using a small plate as a guide.

5. Transfer to greased baking trays. Bake for 15 to 20 minutes in an oven preheated to 350°F/180°C, Gas Mark 4. When ready, the biscuits should be light gold in colour.

6. Dredge with sugar. Cool on a wire rack. Store in an airtight tin when cold.

Chocolate Squares

(Makes 20)

Make as Shrewsbury Biscuits, but reduce the quantity of flour to 7 oz (200 g) and add 1 oz (25 g) cocoa powder in its place. Sift both together into a bowl. Omit the lemon peel and flavour with 1 teaspoon vanilla essence, adding it at the same time as the egg. Roll out thinly and cut into 20 squares. Bake as Shrewsbury Biscuits. Dust with sifted icing sugar. Store in an airtight tin.

Chocolate Sandwich Biscuits

(Makes 10)

Make as Chocolate Squares. Sift icing sugar over 10 biscuits. Spread remainder with Italian-style chocolate nut spread, such as Nutch or Nutella. Place two halves carefully together with icing sugar side uppermost. Store in an airtight tin.

RASPBERRY SANDWICH BISCUITS (Makes 10)

These colourful biscuits are best made and eaten on the same day.

4 oz (125 g) plain flour
2 oz (50 g) butter or block
  margarine
2 oz (50 g) caster sugar
1 oz (25 g) ground almonds
8 to 10 teaspoons well-beaten egg

To complete
Raspberry jam
Icing sugar

1. Sift the flour into a bowl. Cut in the butter or margarine with a knife and rub in finely with the fingertips.

2. Mix in the sugar and almonds.

3. Using a fork, mix to a stiff dough with the egg.

4. Turn on to a floured surface. Knead lightly until smooth.

5. Roll out thinly. Cut into 20 rounds with a 2-inch (5-cm) diameter biscuit cutter, re-rolling and re-cutting trimmings to give the full quantity.

6. Transfer to a lightly buttered baking tray. Bake for 12 minutes in an oven preheated to 400°F/200°C, Gas Mark 6.

7. Remove from the oven. Cool on the tray for about 3 minutes. Carefully transfer biscuits to a wire cooling rack.

8. When completely cold, sandwich together with a thin spread of jam. Dust with icing sugar.

CHRISTMAS STARS

(Makes 30)

Short, crisp biscuits which are well-suited to the festive season.

4 oz (125 g) plain flour
4 oz (125 g) semolina
3 oz (75 g) icing sugar
5 oz (150 g) butter or margarine
½ teaspoon vanilla _or_ almond
  essence
2 to 3 tablespoons beaten egg

1. Sift the dry ingredients into a bowl. Rub in the butter or margarine finely.

2. Mix to a stiff pastry with essence and egg, using a fork to bind the ingredients together. Wrap in foil or cling film and chill for 45 minutes.

3. Turned on to a floured surface. Knead lightly until smooth. Roll out thinly and cut into 30 stars with a biscuit cutter, re-rolling and re-cutting trimmings to get the required number.

4. Transfer to a lightly greased baking tray and bake for about 15 to 20 minutes in an oven preheated to 350°F/180°C, Gas Mark 4. When ready, the biscuits should be straw-coloured.

5. Cool on a wire rack. Store in an airtight tin when cold.

Iced Christmas Stars

(Makes 30)

For glacé icing, sift 8 oz (225 g) icing sugar into a bowl. Mix to a stiff icing with a few teaspoons lemon juice. Spread thinly over the biscuits. If liked, sprinkle icing with toasted coconut or chopped nuts. Leave until set before eating and/or storing.

CHRISTMAS BISCUITS (Makes 14)

With the warm aroma of sugar and spice and all things nice, these are delicious biscuits for any festive season. They are particularly recommended for Hallowe'en, Christmas and even Easter.

4 oz (125 g) plain flour
2 level teaspoons allspice
1 level teaspoon cinnamon
2 oz (50 g) butter or block
  margarine
2 oz (50 g) soft brown sugar
8 to 10 teaspoons well-beaten egg

1. Sift the flour, allspice and cinnamon into a bowl.

2. Cut in the butter or margarine with a knife and then rub it in with the fingertips.

3. Stir in the sugar. Using a fork, mix to a stiff dough with the egg.

4. Draw the mixture together with the fingertips. Turn out on to a floured surface. Knead lightly until smooth.

5. Roll out thinly. Cut into about 14 biscuits with assorted-shaped cutters, re-rolling and re-cutting trimmings to give the required number.

6. Transfer to a lightly greased baking tray. Bake for 12 minutes in an oven preheated to 400°F/200°C, Gas Mark 6.

7. Cool for a few minutes, then transfer to a wire cooling rack. Store in an airtight container when completely cold.

UNROLLED BISCUITS

MACAROON CRUNCHIES (Makes 12)

Lovely, thin biscuits laced with ground almonds and thick honey.

1 egg white (large egg)
¼ teaspoon almond essence
2 oz (50 g) ground almonds
2 oz (50 g) caster sugar
1 level tablespoon thick honey
*1 level tablespoon ground rice or
    semolina*

Topping
6 almonds, blanched and split

1. Line 2 baking trays with Bakewell non-stick parchment paper. Alternatively, use non-stick trays.

2. Place all the ingredients, except the split almonds, in a bowl. Beat until well mixed.

3. Drop teaspoonfuls of the mixture on to the prepared trays. Place them well apart as they spread. Put half an almond on each.

4. Bake for 15 to 20 minutes in an oven preheated to 320°F/160°C, Gas Mark 3. When ready, the biscuits should be pale gold in colour and firm on top.

5. Lift carefully on to a wire rack and leave until cold. Store in an airtight tin.

HONEY CRUNCHIES
(Makes 30)

Adaptable little biscuits-cum-cakes that are ideal for coffee mornings and children's parties.

2 rounded tablespoons clear honey
3 oz (75 g) butter or margarine
2 level teaspoons instant coffee powder
1 tablespoon hot water
6 oz (175 g) icing sugar, sifted
4 oz (125 g) rice krispies

1. Melt the honey and butter or margarine in a saucepan. Remove from the heat.

2. Dissolve the coffee powder in the hot water.

3. Add the coffee, icing sugar and rice krispies to the saucepan.

4. Mix well so that all the rice krispies are coated with the honey mixture and hold together.

5. Spoon into 30 paper cake cases and leave in a cool place to set.

Note
If possible, make and eat these biscuits on the same day.

COCONUT PYRAMIDS (1) (Makes 12)

Coconut Pyramids are quick and easy to make, and they are also fairly economical. This version is based on condensed milk; some variations follow.

4 slightly rounded tablespoons sweetened condensed milk
½ teaspoon vanilla essence
4 oz (125 g) desiccated coconut

1. Line a large baking tray with rice paper.

2. In a bowl, mix the condensed milk with essence and coconut.

3. Shape into 12 pyramids with damp hands. Transfer to the prepared tray.

4. Bake until light gold in colour. This will take about 12 to 15 minutes in an oven preheated to 325°F/160°C, Gas Mark 3.

5. Remove from the oven and cool to lukewarm.

6. Lift pyramids from the tray and trim away surplus rice paper from the bottom of each.

7. Stand pyramids on a wire rack until completely cold. Store in an airtight tin.

COCONUT PYRAMIDS (2)   (Makes 24)

The recipe for these Pyramids, or Coconut Macaroons as they are sometimes called, requires eggs.

8 oz (225 g) desiccated coconut
5 oz (150 g) caster sugar
½ teaspoon vanilla <u>or</u> almond
   essence
2 Grade 3 (standard) eggs

1. Prepare 2 baking trays, as described in Coconut Pyramids (1).

2. Mix together the coconut, sugar, essence and eggs, lightly beaten.

3. Shape into 24 pyramids and place on prepared trays.

4. Bake for about 15 minutes in an oven preheated to 350°F/ 180°C, Gas Mark 4. When ready, the pyramids should be a warm gold colour.

5. Remove from the trays, trim away surplus rice paper from the bottom of each and cool on wire racks. Store in an airtight tin when cold.

COCONUT PYRAMIDS (3) (Makes 12)

When you have a couple of egg whites to spare, this version is well worth making.

2 egg whites
2 oz (50 g) caster sugar
1 oz (25 g) ground rice _or_ potato
   flour
½ teaspoon vanilla essence
4 oz (125 g) desiccated coconut

1. Beat the egg whites until just beginning to foam. Stir in the rest of the ingredients. Mix well.

2. Shape into 12 pyramids. Place on baking trays lined with rice paper.

3. Bake for about 15 minutes, or until golden, in an oven preheated to 350°F/180°C, Gas Mark 4.

4. Remove from trays, trim away the surplus rice paper from the bottom of each pyramid and cool on a wire rack. Store in an airtight tin when cold.

Chocolate Coconut Pyramids (Makes 12)

Follow the recipe for Coconut Pyramids (3), substituting 1 oz (25 g) sifted cocoa powder for the ground rice or potato flour.

Note

If rice paper is unavailable, bake Coconut Pyramids on non-stick trays, or on trays which have been lined with greased foil or Bakewell non-stick parchment paper.

CHOCNUT COOKIES

(Makes 20)

Easy-to-make biscuits, studded with chocolate dots and walnuts and flavoured with vanilla.

3 oz (75 g) butter or block margarine, softened
3 oz (75 g) granulated sugar
3 oz (75 g) soft brown sugar
1 teaspoon vanilla essence
1 Grade 3 (standard) egg, beaten
6 oz (175 g) self-raising flour
2 oz (50 g) walnuts, not too finely chopped
2 oz (50 g) chocolate dots

1. Cream the butter or margarine and the sugars together until light and fluffy.

2. Beat in the essence and egg. Using a fork, mix in the flour, walnuts and chocolate dots.

3. Divide the mixture into 20 pieces and roll into balls. Place them well apart on lightly greased baking trays as they spread.

4. Bake for about 12 to 15 minutes in an oven preheated to 350°F/180°C, Gas Mark 4. When ready, the biscuits should be a pale gold colour.

5. Cool on wire racks. Store in an airtight container when cold.

Chocnut Spice Cookies (Makes 20)

Sift 1 to 2 level teaspoons of mixed spice with the flour. Otherwise, follow the recipe for Chocnut Cookies exactly.

Chocnut Ginger Cookies (Makes 20)

Halve the quantity of nuts to 1 oz (50 g). Include also 1 oz (50 g) finely chopped stem ginger (from a jar in syrup). Otherwise, follow the recipe for Chocnut Cookies exactly.

Choc-Cherry Cookies (Makes 20)

Replace nuts with 2 oz (50 g) finely chopped glacé cherries. Otherwise, follow the recipe for Chocnut Cookies exactly.

MELTING MOMENTS (Makes 20 to 24

Traditional, oat-covered biscuits which, as their name suggest are deliciously short and melting as you bite into them. An they are very easy to make!

4 oz (125 g) butter, softened
3 oz (75 g) caster sugar
1 egg yolk
1 teaspoon vanilla essence
4 oz (125 g) self-raising flour
¼ level teaspoon salt
1 oz (25 g) cornflour
Rolled oats

1. Cream the butter and sugar until very soft and light in colou and texture.

2. Beat in the egg yolk and vanilla essence.

3. Using a fork, work in the flour, first sifted with the salt ar cornflour.

4. Shape the mixture into 20 to 24 small balls, each about tr size of a marble.

5. Toss each ball in oats, tipped on to a piece of foil o greaseproof paper.

6. Transfer to 2 greased baking trays, leaving plenty of roo between each biscuit as they spread.

7. Bake until pale gold, allowing 15 to 20 minutes in an ove preheated to 375°F/190°C, Gas Mark 5.

8. Cool on a wire rack. Store in an airtight tin when cold.

HONEY COOKIES

(Makes 36)

Chewy cookies which, like many others in the book, need no rolling out.

oz (125 g) butter
oz (125 g) soft brown sugar
Grade 3 (standard) egg, beaten
rounded tablespoon clear honey
teaspoon vanilla essence
oz (225 g) self-raising flour,
  sifted

1. Cream the butter and sugar together until light and fluffy.

2. Beat in the egg, honey and essence.

3. Fork in the flour to form a soft paste.

4. Using a teaspoon, place small mounds of the mixture on 3 greased and floured trays, keeping the mounds well apart as they spread.

5. Press the mounds flat with damp fingers and then bake until light brown, allowing 10 to 12 minutes in an oven preheated to 350°F/180°C, Gas Mark 4.

6. Cool to lukewarm, then transfer to wire racks. Store in an airtight tin when completely cold.

Fruit and Spice Honey Cookies

(Makes 36)

Make as Honey Cookies but add 2 oz (50 g) sultanas with the essence. Sift flour with 1 level teaspoon mixed spice.

WINTER COOKIES

(Makes 30)

Ideal for Hallowe'en, these treacle-laced cookies are unusual and very easy to make.

4 oz (125 g) plain flour
1 level teaspoon allspice
½ level teaspoon bicarbonate of soda
1½ oz (40 g) white cooking fat
1½ oz (40 g) soft brown sugar
3 oz (75 g) black treacle
4 tablespoons cold milk soured with 2 teaspoons malt vinegar

1. Sift the flour, allspice and bicarbonate of soda on to a plate.

2. Cream the fat and sugar together until light and fluffy. Beat in the treacle.

3. Using a fork, stir in the flour alternately with the milk and vinegar.

4. When evenly combined, drop small teaspoonfuls of the mixture on to greased baking trays, leaving plenty of room between each as they spread.

5. Bake for 10 to 12 minutes in an oven preheated to 375°F/ 190°C, Gas Mark 5.

6. Cool on a wire rack. Store in an airtight tin when cold.

CORNISH FAIRINGS

(Makes 24)

I always associate these crisp, spicy biscuits with very happy holidays spent in Cornwall.

oz (175 g) plain flour
level teaspoon bicarbonate of
 soda
½ level teaspoons mixed spice
oz (125 g) English Country
Life butter
oz (125 g) soft brown sugar
level teaspoon golden syrup

1. Sift the flour, bicarbonate of soda and spice into a bowl.

2. Place the remaining ingredients in a saucepan. Heat slowly until the butter and syrup melt.

3. Using a fork, gently pour the melted mixture into the dry ingredients and mix well.

4. Shape the mixture into 24 balls. Transfer to 3 buttered baking trays, leaving plenty of room between each ball as they spread.

5. Bake until a warm gold colour, allowing about 15 minutes in an oven preheated to 375°F/190°C, Gas Mark 5.

6. Cool to lukewarm, then transfer to a wire rack. Store in an airtight tin when cold.

MILKY CHOC KRISPIES (Makes 24)

Marvellous uncooked biscuits which are ideal for children's parties—and not too bad for the grown-ups either!

8 oz (225 g) dairy milk
  chocolate
3 oz (75 g) block margarine
2 oz (50 g) caster sugar
2 oz (50 g) cooking dates, finely
  chopped
6 oz (175 g) rice krispies

1. Brush a Swiss roll tin, 11 x 7 inches (27.5 x 17.5 cm), with melted fat. Line the base with Bakewell non-stick parchment paper.

2. Break up the chocolate. Place it in a basin standing over a pan of hot water. Leave until melted, stirring once or twice.

3. Spread the melted chocolate over the base of the tin, completely covering the paper.

4. Melt the margarine in a saucepan. Stir in the sugar and dates. Cook gently for about 5 minutes or until the mixture becomes tacky.

5. Stir in the rice krispies. Spread the mixture evenly into the tin over the chocolate. Cool. Refrigerate when cold to firm the mixture.

6. Cut into 24 squares and lift carefully away from the paper. Store in an airtight tin.

MUESLI 'THINS'

(Makes 40)

Ultra-thin, crisp biscuits which are both elegant and sophisticated. Serve with after-dinner coffee, or with ice cream instead of wafers.

½ oz (115 g) unsweetened
muesli base
level teaspoons currants
level teaspoons chopped nuts
or toasted sunflower seeds
oz (75 g) self-raising flour,
sifted
oz (150 g) caster sugar
oz (150 g) butter, softened
but not runny

1. Tip the muesli base, currants and nuts or sunflower seeds into a bowl.

2. Stir in the flour and sugar. Add the butter and rub it in.

3. Draw the mixture together. Shape into 40 balls, each the size of a marble. Place *no more* than 8 balls on each large baking tray, leaving *plenty* of room between them as they spread.

4. Bake for 10 minutes in an oven preheated to 350°F/180°C, Gas Mark 4. Remove from the oven and leave on the trays for 2 or 3 minutes. Carefully lift off and transfer to a wire cooling rack.

5. When completely cold, store in an airtight container.

MUESLI COOKIES

(Makes 16)

These particular cookies were the result of a reader's enquiry, and they have proved a most popular addition to my own repertoire of wholesome biscuit recipes.

4 oz (125 g) self-raising flour
2 oz (50 g) butter or margarine
  (kitchen temperature)
2 oz (50 g) caster sugar
2 oz (50 g) unsweetened muesli
  base
8 teaspoons well-beaten egg

Glaze
Beaten egg

1. Sift the flour into a bowl. Add the butter or margarine. Cut it in with a knife and rub in with the fingertips until the mixture resembles fine breadcrumbs.

2. Add the sugar and muesli. Using a fork, mix to a stiff paste with beaten egg.

3. Divide the mixture into 16 equal-sized pieces and roll into balls.

4. Place the balls well apart on 2 lightly greased baking trays. Brush with beaten egg. Bake until the biscuits are a pale gold colour, allowing about 12 to 15 minutes in an oven preheated to 400°F/200°C, Gas Mark 6.

5. Cool for 2 or 3 minutes. Transfer to a wire cooling rack. Store in an airtight container when completely cold.

TRADITIONAL FLAPJACK (Cuts into 15 pieces)

These old-fashioned biscuits are favourites with young and old alike.

3 oz (75 g) butter or block margarine
3 oz (75 g) demerara sugar
4 oz (125 g) porridge oats

1. Brush a roasting tin, 9 x 6½ inches (22.5 x 16.25 cm), with melted butter.

2. Place the butter or margarine in a saucepan. Add the sugar. Heat gently until the fat melts.

3. Gradually stir in the oats. Spread evenly into the prepared tin.

4. Bake for 25 to 30 minutes in an oven preheated to 350°F/ 180°C, Gas Mark 4.

5. Remove from the oven and cool for 10 minutes in the tin. Cut into 15 squares. Lift out of the tin and transfer to a cooling rack.

6. Store in an airtight container when completely cold.

RICH FLAPJACK (Cuts into 16 pieces)

This is a more elaborate version of the traditional flapjack.

4 oz (125 g) butter, softened
1 oz (25 g) caster sugar
5 oz (150 g) golden syrup
8 oz (225 g) porridge oats
Large pinch of salt

1. Butter a large Yorkshire pudding tin.

2. Cream the butter and sugar until very light and pale in colour.

3. Stir in the syrup, oats and salt. Spread evenly into the prepared tin.

4. Bake for about 40 minutes in an oven preheated to 350°F/ 180°C, Gas Mark 4, or until the flapjack is a deep gold colour.

5. Remove from the oven and cut into 16 squares or strips. Leave in the tin until cold before removing.

6. Store in an airtight tin.

MOCHA COOKIES

(Makes 16)

These cookies are a cross between a biscuit and a rock cake.

8 oz (225 g) self-raising flour
4 oz (125 g) butter
3 oz (75 g) caster sugar
2 oz (50 g) plain chocolate,
  coarsely chopped
1 Grade 3 (standard) egg, beaten
2 tablespoons liquid coffee
  essence, such as Camp
2 tablespoons milk

1. Sift the flour into a bowl. Rub in the butter until the mixture resembles fine breadcrumbs. Add the sugar and chocolate.

2. Using a fork, mix to a stiff consistency with egg, coffee essence and milk.

3. Spoon 16 small mounds of the mixture on to 2 greased baking trays, leaving space between each as they spread.

4. Bake until they are golden brown, allowing about 20 minutes in an oven preheated to 400°F/200°C, Gas Mark 6.

5. Transfer to a wire cooling rack. Store in an airtight tin when cold.

DUTCH SPRITS BISCUITS (Makes 15)

The word 'sprits', loosely translated, means to squirt and these biscuits are piped or 'squirted' on to baking trays in finger length lines, 'S' shapes or zig-zags. They are pretty biscuits for special occasions.

5 oz (150 g) Dutch unsalted
   butter, softened
4 oz (125 g) caster sugar
7 oz (200 g) plain flour
Pinch of salt
½ teaspoon vanilla essence

Topping
Icing sugar for dusting

1. Cream the butter with the sugar until light and fluffy.

2. Stir in the flour, sifted with the salt. Stir in the vanilla essence. Mix thoroughly to combine.

3. Transfer the mixture to a piping bag fitted with a large star-shaped tube.

4. Pipe about 15 lines, 'S' shapes, zig-zags or round whirls on to a buttered baking tray.

5. Bake until very pale gold, allowing about 30 to 40 minutes in an oven preheated to 300°F/150°C, Gas Mark 2.

6. Leave on the trays for 3 or 4 minutes and then transfer carefully to a wire cooling rack. Store in an airtight tin when cold.

Chocolate Sprits (Makes 15)

If liked, dip half of each Sprit into melted plain chocolate, such as Bournville. Leave to set. Store in an airtight tin.

DUTCH CINNAMON BISCUITS (Makes 12)

These biscuits are beautifully tender and have a lovely spicy flavour.

4 oz (125 g) Dutch unsalted butter, softened
2 oz (50 g) caster sugar
6 oz (175 g) plain flour, sifted
½ level teaspoon cinnamon, sifted

Topping
1 Grade 3 (standard) egg, beaten
1 oz (25 g) blanched almonds, finely chopped
1 level tablespoon granulated sugar

1. Cream the butter and sugar together until light and fluffy.

2. Work in the flour and cinnamon, using a fork to mix.

3. Spread the mixture evenly into an ungreased Swiss roll tin, 11 x 7 inches (27.5 x 17.5 cm).

4. Brush with beaten egg and then prick lightly all over with a fork.

5. Sprinkle with almonds and sugar. Bake until golden brown in an oven preheated to 350°F/180°C, Gas Mark 4. Allow approximately 20 to 25 minutes.

6. Remove from the oven and cool for 5 minutes. Cut into 12 fingers.

7. Remove from the tin when lukewarm and transfer to a wire cooling rack. Store in an airtight tin when cold.

PEANUT BUTTER FLAKES   (Makes 24)

Distinctively flavoured, these biscuits have a very crisp, light texture.

2 oz (50 g) plain flour
¼ level teaspoon bicarbonate of soda
2 oz (50 g) butter or block margarine, softened
1 oz (25 g) sugar
2 oz (50 g) soft brown sugar (light variety)
½ teaspoon vanilla essence
2 oz (50 g) smooth peanut butter
1 Grade 3 (standard) egg

1. Sift the flour and bicarbonate of soda on to a plate.

2. Cream the butter or margarine with both sugars until light and fluffy. Beat in the vanilla essence, peanut butter and the egg.

3. Using a fork, gradually work the flour mixture into the creamed ingredients.

4. Drop teaspoonfuls of mixture, 1 inch (2.5 cm) apart, on to 2 or 3 ungreased baking trays.

5. Bake for 10 to 12 minutes until golden in an oven preheated to 350°F/180°C, Gas Mark 4.

6. Transfer to a wire rack to cool. Store in an airtight tin when cold.

SHORTBREAD SELECTION

There are many kinds of this traditional biscuit which originated in Scotland, and given below is a selection of recipes from which to choose. Usually *no liquid is added* to bind the ingredients together.

BUTTER FINGERS

(Makes 24)

Trouble-free to make, these biscuits are reminiscent of the very best shortbreads both in taste and texture.

4 oz (125 g) butter, softened
2 oz (50 g) caster sugar
5 oz (150 g) plain flour

Topping
Caster sugar

1. Cream the butter and sugar until very light and fluffy.

2. Stir in the flour with a fork. Spread evenly into an ungreased Swiss roll tin measuring 11 x 7 inches (27.5 x 17.5 cm).

3. Ridge into lines, lengthwise, using the prongs of a fork.

4. Bake until pale gold, allowing 20 to 25 minutes in an oven preheated to 350°F/180°C, Gas Mark 4.

5. Cool to lukewarm in the tin, then dredge lightly with caster sugar. Cut into 24 fingers and remove to a wire cooling rack. Store in an airtight tin when cold.

BUTTER SHORTBREAD (Cuts into 8 wedges)

This is a good basic recipe from which to make delicious, crisp Scottish-style shortbread.

5 oz (150 g) plain flour
1 oz (25 g) fine semolina (for added crispness)
2 oz (50 g) caster sugar
4 oz (125 g) unsalted butter

Topping
3 level teaspoons caster sugar

1. Sift the flour into a bowl. Stir in the semolina and sugar.

2. Add the butter. Cut it in with a knife and then rub in with the fingertips.

3. Draw the mixture together to form crumbles. Transfer to an ungreased round sandwich tin, 7 inches (17.5 cm) in diameter.

4. Press out smoothly until the tin is covered with an even layer of biscuit mixture.

5. Spread evenly with a palette knife. Ridge the edges with a fork and then prick all over at regular intervals to give a typical shortbread effect. Sprinkle with sugar.

6. Bake for 1 hour in an oven preheated to 300°F/150°C, Gas Mark 3. The shortbread should be the colour of pale straw.

7. Remove from the oven. Cool to lukewarm and then cut into 8 wedges. Carefully ease out of the tin.

8. Transfer to a wire cooling rack. When completely cold, put into an airtight container.

Butter Shortbread with Almonds   (Cuts into 8 wedges)

Make as Butter Shortbread with semolina, but add 2 oz (50 g)
finely ground blanched and toasted almonds with the sugar.

Melt-in-the-mouth Shortbread   (Cuts into 8 wedges)

The ingredients are exactly the same as for Butter Shortbread,
but the method is different and the result is a much smoother
shortbread with a melt-in-the-mouth texture. Sift the flour into
a bowl. Add the semolina. In a separate bowl, cream the sugar
with slightly softened butter until very light and fluffy and pale
cream in colour. The consistency should resemble whipped
cream. Fork in the flour. When the mixture has been evenly
mixed, spread it into a sandwich tin and continue exactly as
directed for Butter Shortbread.

DUTCH SHORTBREAD (Cuts into 10 wedges)

A classic shortbread from Holland and gloriously rich. If preferred, omit the lemon peel and sift the flour with 1½ level teaspoons of mixed spice.

8 oz (225 g) Dutch unsalted butter (kitchen temperature)
6 oz (175 g) caster sugar
Finely grated peel of 1 washed and dried lemon or 1½ level teaspoons mixed spice
12 oz (350 g) plain flour

Topping
A little unsweetened evaporated milk

1. Cream the butter and sugar together until very light and fluffy. (The consistency should resemble whipped cream.)

2. Stir in the lemon peel, if used, with the flour. Alternatively, sift the spice and flour on to a plate and, using a fork, stir into the creamed mixture.

3. Spread the mixture evenly into an 8-inch (20-cm) ungreased sandwich tin.

4. Make a lattice pattern on top with the prongs of a fork, then brush with evaporated milk.

5. Bake for 45 minutes in an oven preheated to 350°F/180°C, Gas Mark 4.

6. Cool in the tin for 10 minutes. Cut into 10 wedges, lift out carefully and transfer to a wire cooling rack. Store in an airtight tin when completely cold.

GRASMERE SHORTBREAD (Cuts into 10 wedges)

A Lake District speciality—a crumbly, spicy version of traditional shortbread.

8 oz (225 g) plain flour
Large pinch of salt
¼ level teaspoon bicarbonate of soda
1 level teaspoon powdered ginger
4 oz (125 g) butter or block margarine
4 oz (125 g) soft brown sugar

1. Sift the flour, salt, bicarbonate of soda and ginger into a bowl.

2. Rub in the butter or margarine with the fingertips until finely blended. Add the sugar.

3. Sprinkle thickly into an 8-inch (20-cm) buttered sandwich tin, tapping the tin lightly to form an even layer.

4. Smooth the top by pressing lightly downwards with the flat of the hand.

5. Bake in an oven preheated to 300°F/160°C, Gas Mark 3. Allow about 45 minutes, or until the shortbread is firm and pale gold.

6. Cool to lukewarm in the tin, then cut into 10 wedges. Carefully remove to a wire rack. Store in an airtight tin when cold.

DUTCH JANHAGEL

(Makes 20)

Dutch cinnamon biscuits are one of the highlights of ordering a cup of coffee in Holland—one of these biscuits nearly always comes with it!

6 oz (175 g) plain flour
1 level teaspoon cinnamon
2 oz (50 g) caster sugar
4 oz (125 g) Dutch unsalted
  butter

Topping
1 oz (25 g) flaked almonds
1 level tablespoon granulated
  sugar

1. Sift the flour and cinnamon into a bowl. Add the sugar.

2. Rub in the butter. Draw the mixture together with a fork.

3. Spread the mixture into a buttered Swiss roll tin measuring about 11 x 7 inches (27.5 x 17.5 cm), and smooth with a damp knife or palm of the hand.

4. Sprinkle with almonds and sugar. Bake for 20 minutes, or until golden brown, in an oven preheated to 350°F/180°C, Gas Mark 4.

5. Cool to lukewarm, then cut into 20 fingers. Store in an airtight tin when cold.

DUTCH GINGER SHORTCAKE (Makes 24)

For those who like stem ginger, these rich and buttery fingers will be a sheer delight.

1 x 7½-oz (210-g) jar stem ginger in syrup
1 lb (450 g) self-raising flour
8 oz (225 g) Dutch unsalted butter
1 Grade 3 (standard) egg, well beaten

Topping
4 oz (125 g) blanched and halved almonds

1. Drain the ginger and chop. Reserve the syrup.

2. Sift the flour into a bowl. Rub in the butter. Add half the chopped ginger.

3. Stir in the reserved syrup and the egg. Work together with a fork.

4. Spread evenly into a large, buttered Swiss roll tin measuring 13 x 9 inches (32.5 x 22.5 cm).

5. Press the remainder of the chopped ginger and the nuts on top. Bake for 30 to 40 minutes, or until light brown, in an oven preheated to 350°F/180°C, Gas Mark 4.

6. Cool to lukewarm in the tin, then cut into 24 fingers. Transfer to a wire cooling rack. Store in an airtight tin when cold.

SAVOURY BISCUITS

BACON BISCUITS

(Makes 28 to 30)

A surprise package and quite delicious with mid-morning coffee or a cup of tea.

6 oz (175 g) streaky bacon, de-rinded and very finely chopped
6 oz (175 g) butter or block margarine, softened
6 oz (175 g) plain flour
4 oz (125 g) Cheddar or Gouda cheese, finely grated

1. Fry the bacon in its own fat until crisp and golden brown. Drain on paper towels.

2. Beat the butter or margarine until creamy. Using a fork, stir in the flour, cheese and two-thirds of the bacon.

3. Place 28 to 30 teaspoonfuls of the mixture, well apart as they spread, on to 2 greased baking trays.

4. Sprinkle the rest of the bacon over the biscuits. Bake for 30 minutes in an oven preheated to 325°F/160°C, Gas mark 3.

5. Transfer to a wire cooling rack. Leave until cold. Store for up to one week in an airtight container in the refrigerator.

SAVOURY TWISTS

(Makes 30)

Appetising savoury biscuits which are ideal for cocktail parties.

4 oz (125 g) plain flour
¼ level teaspoon salt
¼ level teaspoon paprika
⅛ level teaspoon cayenne pepper
   (fiery, so be careful)
⅛ level teaspoon garlic granules
2½ oz (65 g) butter or margarine
About 6 teaspoons beaten egg

Filling
Tubed or canned tomato purée
Celery salt

1. Sift the dry ingredients into a bowl. Rub in the butter or margarine with the fingertips until finely blended.

2. Mix to a fairly stiff dough with water. Turn on to a floured surface. Knead lightly until smooth and wrap in foil or cling film. Refrigerate for 30 minutes.

3. Roll out thinly into a rectangle measuring 12 x 8 inches (30 x 20 cm).

4. Spread thinly with tomato purée to within ½ inch (1.25 cm) of the edges, then sprinkle lightly with celery salt.

5. Brush the edges with water, then fold the pastry in half to form a rectangle measuring 6 x 8 inches (15 x 20 cm).

6. Press lightly with a rolling pin, then cut into approximately 30 strips, each 3 inches (7.5 cm) in length.

7. Twist each strip and place on a well-buttered baking tray. Bake for about 12 to 15 minutes in an oven preheated to 425°F/220°C, Gas Mark 7.

8. Cool on a wire rack. Store in an airtight tin when cold.

CHEESE ASSORTMENT

Take one recipe and make four different biscuits. This is always acceptable as it saves a good deal of time and trouble and slots into the category of 'batch baking'—ideal for busy housewives who may like to spend one day a week in the kitchen cooking and baking for the week, or weeks, ahead.

12 oz (350 g) plain flour
1 level teaspoon salt
1/4 level teaspoon white pepper
1 level teaspoon dry mustard
1/2 level teaspoon paprika
8 oz (225 g) butter or margarine
8 oz (225 g) very finely grated Cheddar cheese (stale and dry cheese is best)
2 egg yolks
Cold water

1. Sift the dry ingredients into a bowl.

2. Rub in the butter or margarine until finely blended. Add the cheese.

3. Mix to a stiff (but not too crumbly) dough with egg yolks and water, using a fork to gather the ingredients together.

4. Turn on to a floured surface and knead lightly until smooth

5. Foil-wrap or wrap in cling film and refrigerate for 1 hour

6. Unwrap and divide the pastry into 4 equal portions.

Cheese Straws (Makes 3 to 4 dozen)

portion of pastry

1. Roll out first portion of pastry thinly. Cut into 36 to 48 strips, 3 inches (7.5 cm) in length. Arrange strips carefully on lightly greased baking trays.

2. Re-roll the pastry trimmings and cut into 2-inch (5-cm) rings with biscuit cutters. Place on the trays.

3. Bake until pale gold, allowing about 7 to 10 minutes in an oven preheated to 450°F/230°C, Gas Mark 8.

4. Remove carefully to wire racks and leave to cool.

5. To serve, thread the straws through the rings to look like bales of hay. Store in an airtight tin.

Morning Coffee Biscuits (Makes 12 to 14)

portion of pastry

1. Roll out second portion of pastry and cut 12 or 14 rounds with a 2-inch (5-cm) plain biscuit cutter. Transfer to 1 or 2 greased baking trays.

2. Bake as for Cheese Straws, allowing about 12 minutes.

3. Cool on a wire rack. Store in an airtight tin.

1 portion of pastry

Cheese cream
3 oz (75 g) butter, softened
2 oz (50 g) very finely grated
    Cheddar cheese
Salt
Pepper
½ level teaspoon prepared
    mustard

Topping
Paprika <u>or</u> finely chopped parsley

1 portion of pastry
Cheese cream, as given for Cheese
    Butterflies above

Cheese Butterflies (Makes 12 to 14)

1. Roll out third portion of pastry thinly and cut into 24 to 28 rounds with a 1-inch (2.5-cm) plain biscuit cutter.

2. Cut 12 to 14 rounds in half to form 'wings'. Transfer to greased baking trays.

3. Bake exactly as for Cheese Straws. Cool on wire racks.

4. To serve, make up cheese cream by beating together the butter, cheese, salt and pepper to taste and the mustard. Pipe or spoon whirls of the cheese cream on to the whole biscuits, then top with 'wings' to resemble butterflies in flight.

5. Dust lightly with paprika or finely chopped parsley.

Cheese Sandwich Biscuits (Makes 12 to 1

1. Roll out fourth portion of pastry thinly and cut into 24 to 2 rounds with a 1-inch (2.5-cm) plain biscuit cutter.

2. Bake exactly as for Cheese Straws. Cool on wire racks.

3. To serve, sandwich together with cheese cream.

APPETISER PUFFS

(Makes 18)

Tasty and welcome with long cool drinks, these salt-topped biscuits store well and are useful to keep in reserve for unexpected guests.

oz (150 g) plain flour
oz (25 g) instant potato powder
level teaspoon dry mustard
level teaspoon salt
oz (75 g) butter or margarine
oz (75 g) stale Cheddar cheese,
very finely grated
to 4 tablespoons cold water

opping
ld milk
arse sea salt

1. Sift the flour, potato powder, mustard and salt into a bowl. Rub in the butter or margarine.

2. Add the cheese. Using a fork, mix to a stiff paste with cold water.

3. Turn on to a floured surface and knead lightly until smooth.

4. Roll out thinly and cut into 18 rounds with a 2-inch (5-cm) plain biscuit cutter, re-rolling and re-cutting trimmings to give required quantity.

5. Transfer to greased baking trays. Brush with milk and sprinkle with salt.

6. Bake until lightly browned, allowing about 8 to 10 minutes in an oven preheated to 400°F/200°C, Gas Mark 6.

7. Cool on wire racks. Store in an airtight tin when cold.

CHEESE AND WALNUT BISCUITS (Makes 32)

Very Italian in character, these are sophisticated, savoury biscuits with a deliciously nutty flavour.

8 oz (225 g) plain flour
½ level teaspoon salt
6 oz (175 g) butter or margarine
2 oz (50 g) very finely grated Parmesan cheese
2 oz (50 g) walnuts, very finely chopped
1 egg yolk
1 tablespoon cold water

Topping
1 egg white

1. Sift the flour and salt into a bowl. Rub in the butter or margarine with the fingertips until finely blended. Add two thirds of the cheese and the same amount of nuts.

2. Using a fork, mix to a stiff dough with egg yolk and water. Draw together to form a ball. Wrap in foil or cling film and refrigerate for 1 hour.

3. Roll out on a floured surface to a thickness of ¼ inch (5 mm). Cut into about 32 rounds with a 2-inch (5-cm) fluted biscuit cutter.

4. Transfer to lightly greased trays. Brush with egg white whipped until just foamy. Sprinkle with the rest of the cheese and nuts.

5. Bake until pale gold, allowing 25 minutes in an oven preheated to 350°F/180°C, Gas Mark 4.

6. Cool on wire racks. Store in an airtight tin when cold.

LUNCH-BOX PEANUT BARS (Makes 12)

Packed with cheese and topped with nuts, these shortbread-style savoury bars are perfect for packed meals and should be especially popular with children. Block margarine may be used instead of butter but expect a somewhat different flavour.

oz (175 g) butter, softened
oz (225 g) plain flour, sifted
level teaspoon dry mustard, sifted
oz (175 g) Cheddar cheese, finely grated

Topping
oz (50 g) salted peanuts

1. Cream the butter until light. Stir in the flour, mustard and cheese.

2. Draw the mixture together with the hands. Spread evenly into a Swiss roll tin measuring 11 x 7 inches (27.5 x 17.5 cm).

3. Sprinkle with peanuts and press down with the flat of the hand to keep them in position.

4. Bake until pale gold, allowing 1 hour in an oven preheated to 325°F/160°C, Gas Mark 3.

5. Cool to lukewarm, then cut into 12 bars. Carefully lift on to a wire cooling rack. Store in an airtight tin when cold.

SESAME CHEESE FINGERS (Makes 40)

Well-suited to the cocktail hour, these savoury biscuits are piquant and crackly and store well in a biscuit tin.

6 oz (175 g) plain flour
1 level teaspoon salt
4 oz (125 g) butter
2 to 3 tablespoons cold milk

Filling
2 level tablespoons mild prepared
   mustard
1 rounded tablespoon toasted
   sesame seeds
2 oz (50 g) very finely grated
   Cheddar cheese

Topping
Beaten egg
Paprika

1. Sift the flour and salt into a bowl. Rub in the butter finely. Mix to a stiff dough with milk.

2. Knead on a lightly floured surface until smooth. Wrap in foil or cling film and refrigerate for 30 minutes.

3. Cut into 2 equal-sized portions. Roll each into a 9-inch (22.5-cm) square. Place 1 portion on a greased tray.

4. Spread the first portion with mustard, then sprinkle with sesame seeds and cheese. Cover with the second portion of pastry.

5. Press down lightly with a rolling pin. Brush with egg and sprinkle with paprika.

6. Bake until golden brown, allowing 10 to 12 minutes in an oven preheated to 400°F/200°C, Gas Mark 6.

7. Leave until lukewarm. Cut into fingers and transfer to a wire cooling rack. Store in an airtight tin when cold.

Caraway Cheese Fingers (Makes 40)

Make as Sesame Cheese Fingers, but sprinkle with cheese only and omit the sesame seeds. Before baking, brush with egg and sprinkle with 1 rounded teaspoon of caraway seeds instead of paprika.

DANISH BLUE CHEESE STRAWS (Makes 50)

A highly original idea from Denmark and a delicious appetiser.

4 oz (125 g) plain flour
¼ level teaspoon salt
1 oz (25 g) lard or white
    cooking fat
1 oz (25 g) Danish butter
6 to 8 teaspoons cold water

Filling
2 oz (50 g) Danish Blue cheese

1. Sift the flour and salt into a bowl. Rub in the fats.

2. Mix to a stiff paste with water. Turn on to a floured surface. Knead lightly until smooth.

3. Roll out thinly into a thin rectangle measuring about 12 x 8 inches (30 x 20 cm).

4. Grate the cheese and use to coat one half of the rolled pastry Fold and cover with the second half.

5. Re-roll the pastry until very thin and the pattern of the cheese just begins to show through.

6. Cut into narrow strips, 3 inches (7.5 cm) in length. Transfer to buttered baking trays.

7. Bake until light brown, allowing about 10 minutes in an oven preheated to 400°F/200°C, Gas Mark 6.

8. Cool on a wire rack. Store in an airtight tin when cold.

DEVILLED TRIANGLES (Makes 20)

These are tasty biscuits which can be eaten for supper with wedges of cheese or hard-boiled eggs and salad.

8 oz (225 g) plain flour
1/2 level teaspoon hot curry powder
1 level teaspoon dry mustard
1 level teaspoon salt
1/2 level teaspoon celery salt
1/2 level teaspoon paprika
5 oz (150 g) butter or margarine
2 oz (50 g) mature Cheddar cheese, grated
1 Grade 3 (standard) egg, well beaten
1 1/2 to 2 tablespoons cold water

Topping
Beaten egg or milk
2 rounded tablespoons salted peanuts, finely chopped

1. Sift all the dry ingredients into a bowl. Rub in the butter or margarine.

2. Add the cheese. Mix to a stiff paste with egg and water.

3. Turn on to a floured surface. Knead lightly until smooth. Divide in half.

4. Roll out each half into a 10-inch (25-cm) round, using a dinner plate as a guide.

5. Cut each circle into 10 triangles. Transfer to 2 well-greased trays. Brush with egg or milk. Sprinkle with nuts.

6. Bake until light brown, allowing 12 to 15 minutes in an oven preheated to 400°F/200°C, Gas Mark 6.

7. Transfer to wire cooling racks. Store in an airtight tin when cold.

Cocktail Triangles (Makes 40)

Make as above but cut each round into 20 triangles.

SAVOURY OAT WEDGES (Makes 10)

A tea-time special for children who prefer savoury biscuits to sweet ones.

8 oz (225 g) self-raising flour
1 level teaspoon paprika
1 level teaspoon salt
½ level teaspoon onion or celery salt
4 oz (125 g) rolled oats
6 oz (175 g) butter or margarine
1 teaspoon Worcestershire sauce
5 tablespoons cold water

1. Sift the flour, paprika and both salts into a bowl. Add the oats.

2. Rub in the butter or margarine with the fingertips until finely blended. Mix to a stiff dough with Worcestershire sauce mixed with the cold water. Add a few extra teaspoons of water if the mixture seems rather dry.

3. Spread into a greased sandwich tin, 8 inches (20 cm) in diameter. Smooth evenly with a knife.

4. Bake for 30 minutes, or until golden, in an oven preheated to 375°F/190°C, Gas Mark 5.

5. Cool to lukewarm in the tin, then cut into 10 wedges. Transfer carefully to a wire rack. Store in an airtight tin when cold.

LIVER PÂTÉ FINGERS (Makes 30)

Served warm from the oven, these fingers will be more than welcome as a mid-morning or early evening snack.

8 oz (225 g) plain flour
½ level teaspoon salt
¼ level teaspoon dry mustard
4 oz (125 g) butter or margarine
1 egg yolk
1½ to 2 tablespoons cold milk

Filling
4 oz (225 g) soft liver pâté
1 tablespoon single cream

Topping
1 egg white
Sesame seeds

1. Sift the flour, salt and mustard into a bowl. Rub in the butter or margarine until the mixture resembles fine breadcrumbs.

2. Mix to a stiff dough with egg yolk and milk, stirring with a fork to draw the ingredients together. Wrap in foil or cling film and refrigerate for 30 minutes.

3. Divide the pastry into 2 equal pieces. Roll out each piece into a 10 x 9-inch (25 x 22.5-cm) rectangle.

4. Beat the pâté with the cream until very smooth. Spread over 1 portion of pastry. Cover with second portion. Press down.

5. Trim away uneven edges. Cut the pâté sandwich into 30 fingers. Place on buttered baking trays. Brush the tops with lightly beaten egg white. Sprinkle lightly with sesame seeds.

6. Bake until pale gold in an oven preheated to 400°F/200°C, Gas Mark 6. Allow about 20 minutes.

7. Cool on a wire rack. Store leftovers for up to 1 week in an airtight container in the refrigerator.

CHEESY OAT CRISPS (Makes 30)

These very savoury biscuits are equally good with a mid-morning cup of coffee or a hot drink at night.

6 oz (175 g) self-raising flour
½ level teaspoon dry mustard
½ level teaspoon salt
¼ level teaspoon white pepper
2 oz (50 g) porridge oats
4½ oz (140 g) white cooking fat
2 oz (50 g) mature Cheddar
   cheese, finely grated
3 to 4 tablespoons cold milk

1. Sift the flour, mustard, salt and pepper into a bowl. Add the oats.

2. Rub in the fat until finely blended, then add the cheese. Using a fork, mix to a stiff dough with the milk.

3. Turn on to a lightly floured board. Knead lightly until smooth and crack-free.

4. Roll out thinly and cut into approximately 30 fingers.

5. Transfer carefully to 2 well-greased baking trays.

6. Bake until the biscuits are golden and crisp, allowing 10 to 12 minutes in an oven preheated to 425°F/220°C, Gas Mark 7.

7. Cool on a wire rack. Store in an airtight tin when cold.

DEVILLED CARAWAY STICKS (Makes 24)

These rather hot biscuits are excellent served with drinks before a meal.

4 oz (125 g) self-raising flour
½ level teaspoon salt
½ level teaspoon dry mustard
¼ level teaspoon freshly milled black pepper
¼ level teaspoon Cayenne pepper (hot!)
½ level teaspoon paprika
2 oz (50 g) butter
1 oz (25 g) mature Cheddar cheese, finely grated
1 egg yolk
6 teaspoons cold milk
1 teaspoon Worcestershire sauce

Topping
1 egg white
Caraway seeds

1. Sift the flour, salt, mustard and peppers into a bowl. Rub in the butter until finely blended. Add the cheese.

2. Mix to a stiff dough with the egg yolk, milk and Worcestershire sauce, beaten together. Draw together with the fingertips.

3. Turn on to a floured surface. Knead lightly until smooth. Roll out thinly. Cut into 24 sticks, each measuring about 6 x 1 inch (15 x 2.5 cm).

4. Transfer the sticks to greased baking trays. Brush with lightly beaten egg white, then sprinkle with caraway seeds.

5. Bake until the biscuits are golden brown and crisp, allowing about 10 minutes in an oven preheated to 400°F/200°C, Gas Mark 6.

6. Remove from the oven and cool on wire racks. Store in an airtight tin when cold.

POPPY SEED SANDWICH BISCUITS (Makes 30)

Appetising little biscuits which go well with an aperitif.

6 oz (175 g) self-raising flour
½ level teaspoon salt
½ level teaspoon dry mustard
¼ level teaspoon celery salt
½ level teaspoon onion salt
2 oz (50 g) semolina
4 oz (125 g) butter or block margarine
2½ to 3 tablespoons cold milk

Filling
A little beaten egg
1 level tablespoon poppy seeds

1. Sift the flour, salt, mustard and both salts into a bowl. Add the semolina.

2. Rub in the butter or margarine until finely blended. Mix to a stiff dough with the milk, stirring with a fork to draw the ingredients together.

3. Turn on to a lightly floured surface. Knead quickly until smooth. Roll out into a thin oblong.

4. Brush one half of the pastry with beaten egg. Sprinkle with poppy seeds. Fold over the other half so that the seeds are sandwiched between 2 pieces of pastry.

5. Re-roll thinly. Cut into about 30 rounds with a 1½-inch (4-cm) plain biscuit cutter. Transfer to greased baking trays. Brush tops with beaten egg.

6. Bake until golden brown and slightly risen, allowing about 12 to 15 minutes in an oven preheated to 375°F/190°C, Gas Mark 5.

7. Cool on a wire rack. Store in an airtight container when completely cold.

PETIT FOURS

MOCHA KISSES (Makes 10)

Rich and luxurious sandwich biscuits for special occasions.

3 oz (75 g) Dutch Wheelbarrow
    butter
3 oz (75 g) caster sugar
4 oz (125 g) plain flour
½ oz (15 g) cocoa powder
1 level teaspoon baking powder
1 tablespoon cold milk

Filling
2 oz (50 g) Dutch Wheelbarrow
    butter
3 oz (75 g) icing sugar, sifted
2 rounded teaspoons instant
    coffee powder
2 to 3 teaspoons milk

Topping
Extra icing sugar, sifted

1. To make the biscuits, cream the butter and sugar well together.

2. Sift together the flour, cocoa powder and baking powder. Using a fork, stir the dry ingredients into the creamed mixture alternately with the milk.

3. Place 20 teaspoonfuls of the mixture, spaced well apart, on buttered trays.

4. Bake for 20 minutes in an oven preheated to 375°F/190°C, Gas Mark 5. Cool on a wire rack.

5. To make the filling, cream all the ingredients well together.

6. Spread the filling over the flat sides of the biscuits. Sandwich together. Dust with icing sugar.

7. Store for up to 1 week in an airtight container in the refrigerator.

NUTTY CINNAMON CRESCENTS (Makes 12)

Somewhat Middle-Eastern in character, these rich little crescents are aromatic and not over-sweet—they simply melt in the mouth!

8 oz (225 g) plain flour
4 oz (125 g) butter
2 level tablespoons caster sugar
2½ to 3 tablespoons single cream

Filling
2 oz (50 g) flaked almonds,
    lightly toasted
1 rounded teaspoon powdered
    cinnamon
1 egg yolk
1 oz (25 g) caster sugar

Topping
Lightly beaten egg white
Icing sugar

1. To make the pastry, sift the flour into a bowl. Add the butter and cut it in with a knife.

2. Rub in the butter with the fingertips until the mixture resembles fine breadcrumbs. Add the sugar. Mix to a stiff dough with the cream.

3. Turn on to a floured surface. Knead lightly until smooth. Cut into 2 portions of equal size.

4. Roll out each portion separately into a 10-inch (25-cm) round. Cut each round into 6 triangles with a sharp knife.

5. To make the filling, coarsely chop the nuts, then mix them with cinnamon, egg yolk and sugar.

6. Spoon equal amounts of the filling on to the widest part of the pastry triangles.

7. Brush the edges of the pastry with water, then roll up each triangle. Curve to form a crescent shape.

8. Place the crescents on a buttered baking tray and brush with egg white.

9. Bake for 25 minutes in an oven preheated to 400°F/200°C, Gas Mark 6.

10. Remove from the oven and transfer to a wire cooling rack. Sift sugar over each and eat when cold.

Note
If possible, make and eat these biscuits on the same day.

ITALIAN AMORETTI

(Makes 18)

Meringue-like, elegant confections, which can double as after-dinner petit fours. It is *essential* to line the baking trays with either edible rice paper or Bakewell non-stick parchment paper, otherwise the biscuits will stick.

2 large egg whites (Grade 1 or
    2 eggs)
Few drops of lemon juice
4 oz (125 g) caster sugar
2 oz (50 g) semolina
2½ oz (65 g) ground almonds
½ teaspoon each, almond and
    vanilla essence
1 oz (25 g) blanched and skinned
    almonds

Filling
Chocolate hazelnut spread,
    such as Nutella or Nutch or
    apricot jam

1. Line 3 shallow, well-buttered baking trays with rice paper or Bakewell non-stick parchment paper.

2. Beat the egg whites and lemon juice to a stiff snow.

3. Gradually add the sugar, beating continually, until the meringue is shiny and firm and forms tall peaks when the beaters are lifted out of the bowl.

4. Using a fork, gently stir in the semolina, almonds and essences. Do not beat.

5. Drop 12 small mounds of the mixture on to each of the prepared trays, allowing plenty of room between each mound as they spread slightly.

6. Chop the blanched almonds and sprinkle them over the biscuits.

7. Bake for 25 to 30 minutes in an oven preheated to 325°F/160°C, Gas Mark 3. When ready, the biscuits should be a pale gold colour.

8. Lift the biscuits off the trays. (Rice paper will come away with each biscuit.) Trim away any surplus rice paper. Cool on a wire rack.

9. When completely cold, sandwich together with chocolate hazelnut filling or jam. Store in an airtight container.

CRUMBLES

(Makes 24)

Chocolate almond petit fours based on a meringue mixture.

2 egg whites (Grade 3 eggs)
1½ teaspoons lemon juice
2½ oz (65 g) icing sugar, sifted
3 oz (75 g) milk flake bars,
    crumbled
1 rounded tablespoon semolina
4 oz (125 g) blanched almonds,
    cut into thin slivers

Coating
3 oz (75 g) plain chocolate
½ oz (15 g) butter

1. Line 3 buttered baking trays with rice paper or Bakewell non-stick parchment paper.

2. Beat the egg whites and lemon juice to a stiff snow.

3. Gradually add the sugar, beating continually, until the meringue is very thick and shiny and stands in tall peaks when the beaters are lifted out of the bowl.

4. Using a large metal spoon, gently fold in the crumbled flake bars, semolina and almonds.

5. Place 8 teaspoonfuls of meringue mixture on each prepared baking tray, leaving plenty of room between each mound of meringue.

6. Flatten with a knife dipped in cold water.

7. Bake until pale gold and crisp, allowing about 25 minutes in an oven preheated to 300°F/150°C, Gas Mark 2.

8. Remove from the oven, cool slightly and lift carefully off the trays. The rice paper will come away as well, so trim away the surplus round the edges of each biscuit. Cool completely on wire racks.

9. To make the coating, break up the chocolate and place, with the butter, in a basin standing over a pan of gently simmering water.

10. Leave until melted, stirring once or twice. Spread over the rice paper side of each biscuit. Leave until set before eating.

11. Store leftovers in an airtight tin away from heat.

FLORENTINES

These are the most expensive of biscuits to buy, but quite the opposite if home-made. Florentines are always a treat at tea-time or if served with after-dinner ice cream sundaes instead of wafers.

3 oz (75 g) butter
4 tablespoons single cream
4 oz (125 g) icing sugar, sifted
1½ oz (40 g) plain flour
3 oz (75 g) chopped mixed peel
2 oz (50 g) glacé cherries, chopped
2 oz (50 g) flaked almonds
1 teaspoon lemon juice

Coating
4 oz (125 g) plain chocolate

1. Line 2 large, well-buttered baking trays with rice paper making sure there are no gaps. Alternatively, use Bakewell non-stick parchment paper.

2. Place the butter, cream and sugar in a saucepan. Heat gently until the butter melts.

3. Remove from the heat. Stir in all the remaining ingredients except the chocolate. Leave until cold.

4. Spoon equal amounts of the mixture on to the prepared trays, leaving plenty of room between each mound as they spread.

5. Bake for about 10 minutes, or until pale gold, in an oven preheated to 375°F/190°C, Gas Mark 5.

6. Leave to cool to lukewarm. Carefully remove from the trays and trim away the ragged edges of rice paper. Cool completely on wire racks.

7. To make the coating, break up the chocolate. Melt it slowly in a basin over hot water.

8. Spread over the rice paper sides of the Florentines and leave until half-set. Mark in wavy lines with the prongs of a fork.

9. Return to wire racks. Leave until the chocolate has set before eating.

10. Store in an airtight tin in a cool place.

Florentine Petit Fours (Makes 24)

For tiny biscuits which you can serve with coffee after a meal, drop 24 mounds of the mixture on to prepared trays. Bake and coat with chocolate as directed above.

SPECIALITY BISCUITS

VIENNA BISCUITS

(Makes 2

A very special treat for very special occasions.

*3 oz (75 g) hazelnuts, finely
  ground*
6 oz (175 g) butter, softened
2 oz (50 g) icing sugar, sifted
6 oz (175 g) plain flour, sifted

Coating
4 oz (125 g) plain chocolate
½ oz (15 g) butter
*2 teaspoons instant coffee powder
  dissolved in 2 teaspoons hot
  water*

1. Beat the butter to a cream. Stir in the nuts, sugar and flou
using a fork to mix well.

2. Draw the mixture together and wrap in foil or cling film
Chill in the refrigerator for 1 hour.

3. Roll out thinly on a floured surface. Cut into about 20 roun
with a 3-inch (7.5-cm) biscuit cutter, re-rolling and re-cutti
the trimmings to give the required amount.

4. Transfer to baking trays. Bake for 20 minutes in an ov
preheated to 325°F/160°C, Gas Mark 3. Cool on a wire rac

5. To coat, melt the chocolate and butter in a basin over h
water. Stir in the coffee.

6. Spread the coating over the biscuits. Leave to set befo
eating. When cold, store in an airtight tin away from heat.

MACAROONS

(Makes 12 to 14)

Traditional and almond-packed, macaroons are still a great favourite. They are perfect for Easter and Christmas, when a dozen or so boxed prettily makes a highly acceptable gift.

egg whites (large eggs)
oz (125 g) ground almonds
oz (125 g) caster sugar
oz (15 g) cornflour or semolina
teaspoon almond essence
teaspoon vanilla essence

•pping
little extra egg white
o 7 blanched almonds, split

1. Brush 2 large baking trays with melted butter. Line completely with rice paper, or Bakewell non-stick parchment paper, making sure there are no gaps.

2. Lightly whisk the egg whites but do *not* allow them to stiffen. Stir in the remaining main ingredients. Mix well.

3. Pipe or spoon small mounds of the mixture on to the prepared trays. Flatten the mounds slightly with a damp knife.

4. Brush with beaten egg white. Top each mound with an almond half.

5. Bake for 20 to 25 minutes in an oven preheated to 325°F/160°C, Gas Mark 3. When ready, the macaroons should be a light gold colour.

6. Cool slightly on the trays, then lift off.

7. Trim away the surplus rice paper (which will look ragged) from round the edge of each macaroon, then cool on a wire rack.

8. Store in an airtight tin when cold.

DANISH BISCUIT SELECTION

Danish housewives are well-known for their baking and here
a selection of typical and traditional biscuits to augment t
biscuit tin. They have all been made with Danish butter and a
other butter, or margarine, may give different results.

BASIC BUTTER BISCUITS (Makes 5

This is a basic recipe for 3 varieties of biscuits.

8 oz (225 g) plain flour
½ level teaspoon baking powder
6 oz (175 g) Danish butter
4 oz (125 g) granulated sugar
½ teaspoon vanilla essence
1 Grade 2 (large) egg, well beaten
Cold milk, if necessary

1. Sift the flour and baking powder into a bowl. Rub in t
butter with the fingertips until the mixture resembles fi
breadcrumbs.

2. Add the sugar to the rubbed-in ingredients. Using a fo
mix to a fairly stiff dough with essence, egg and milk,
necessary.

3. Turn on to a lightly floured surface. Knead until smoo
Divide into 3 equal portions.

Jewish 'Cakes'

(Makes 22)

ortion of basic biscuit dough

pping
ten egg
ounded tablespoon blanched
lmonds, finely chopped
vel tablespoon caster sugar
vel teaspoon cinnamon

1. Roll out the dough very thinly on a floured surface. Cut into 22 rounds with a 2-inch (5-cm) plain biscuit cutter, re-rolling and re-cutting trimmings to make required quantity.

2. Transfer to lightly buttered trays. Brush with egg, then sprinkle with almonds, sugar and cinnamon.

3. Bake for 8 to 9 minutes in an oven preheated to 375°F/190°C, Gas Mark 5. When ready, the biscuits should be a light gold colour.

4. Cool on a wire rack. Store in an airtight tin when cold.

Vanilla Rings

(Makes 2

1 portion of basic biscuit dough
1 oz (25 g) Danish butter, softened
1 oz (25 g) ground almonds
½ teaspoon vanilla essence

1. Place the dough in a bowl and knead in the rest of t ingredients to form a soft dough.

2. Transfer to an icing bag fitted with a star-shaped pipe.

3. Pipe 22 rings of mixture, each about 2 inches (5 cm) diameter, on to lightly buttered trays.

4. Bake until the rings are a light gold, allowing about 9 minu in an oven preheated to 375°F/190°C, Gas Mark 5.

5. Cool on a wire rack. Store in an airtight tin when cold.

Finnish 'Bread' (Makes 10)

portion of basic biscuit dough

opping
  little beaten egg
  level tablespoon caster sugar

1. Roll the dough into a 'sausage' shape, about 1 inch (2.5 cm) in diameter. Square off by pressing the rounded sides to flatten them slightly.

2. Cut into 10 ½-inch (1.25-cm) slices on the diagonal. Arrange on buttered trays.

3. Brush with egg, then sprinkle with sugar. Bake until pale gold in colour, allowing 10 minutes at 375°F/190°C, Gas Mark 5.

4. Cool on a wire rack. Store in an airtight tin when cold.

DANISH LACE CAKES

(Makes 15)

These look like miniature doyleys and may be served for tea or as an accompaniment to ice cream sundaes.

4 oz (125 g) Danish butter, softened
4 oz (125 g) granulated sugar
4 oz (125 g) rolled oats
½ teaspoon vanilla essence

1. Cream the butter and sugar together until light and fluffy.

2. Stir in the oats and vanilla.

3. Roll into 15 balls. Transfer to buttered baking trays, leaving plenty of room between each as they spread.

4. Flatten each ball slightly, then bake until they are a golden brown, allowing 5 to 6 minutes in an oven preheated to 400°F/200°C, Gas Mark 6.

5. Leave to cool slightly on the baking trays, then transfer carefully to wire racks. Store in an airtight tin when cold.

Spicy Lace Cakes

(Makes 15)

Use ½ teaspoon mixed spice instead of vanilla essence.

DANISH BROWN CAKES

(Makes 30)

These are Denmark's version of refrigerator biscuits—spicy slices cut from a roll of dough which has been wrapped and kept cold until needed. The advantage here is that you can slice and bake a few biscuits at a time, storing the remainder of the roll in the refrigerator for another occasion. Of course, the entire roll may be cut up and all the biscuits baked at once.

oz (125 g) Danish butter
oz (125 g) soft brown sugar
oz (50 g) golden syrup
level teaspoon cream of tartar
teaspoon water
oz (25 g) blanched almonds, finely chopped
oz (25 g) chopped mixed peel
oz (225 g) plain flour
level teaspoons mixed spice or allspice

pping
aked almonds

1. Cream the butter and sugar together until light and fluffy. Beat in the syrup.

2. Mix the cream of tartar with the water and add to the creamed ingredients with the almonds and peel.

3. Using a fork, gradually add the flour sifted with the mixed spice or allspice.

4. Shape into a roll, 2 inches (5 cm) in diameter, and wrap in foil or cling film. Refrigerate for 2 hours.

5. Unwrap. Slice off the required number of biscuits and place them on buttered trays. Top each with a piece of flaked almond.

6. Bake until lightly browned, allowing 6 to 7 minutes in an oven preheated to 400°F/200°C, Gas Mark 6.

7. Cool on a wire rack. Store in an airtight tin when cold.

DANISH BUTTER FANS (Makes 24)

Melt-in-the-mouth biscuits for special occasions.

5 oz (150 g) Danish butter,
  softened
2 oz (50 g) caster sugar
4 oz (125 g) plain flour
2 oz (50 g) self-raising flour
1 oz (25 g) cornflour
¼ teaspoon vanilla essence

Topping
Caster sugar

1. Place all the ingredients in a bowl. Work together with the fingers until the mixture holds together and forms a dough. Wrap in foil or cling film and refrigerate for 1 hour.

2. Divide the dough into 3 equal pieces. Roll each out into a 7 inch (17.5-cm) circle, using a plate as a guide.

3. Cut each round into 8 triangles. Transfer carefully to floured baking trays.

4. Dust the tops with caster sugar. Bake for 15 to 20 minutes, or until pale gold, in an oven preheated to 325°F/160°C, Gas Mark 3.

5. Leave for 5 minutes, then remove carefully to wire racks. Store in an airtight tin when cold.

Petticoat Tails (Makes 24)

Roll out the 3 x 7-inch (17.5-cm) rounds as described above. Cut out the centres with a 1-inch (2.5-cm) plain biscuit cutter. Ridge the outside edges with the prongs of a fork. Cut each round into 8 triangles or 'petticoats'. Bake as above.

DANISH CHOC COOKIES (Makes 40)

Easy-to-make biscuits, decorated rather attractively with glacé cherries.

oz (150 g) Danish butter,
  softened
oz (75 g) icing sugar, sifted
oz (175 g) plain flour
Grade 3 (standard) egg, beaten
oz (50 g) chocolate dots
oz (50 g) unblanched almonds,
  chopped

Topping
0 glacé cherries, quartered

1. Lightly cream together the butter and sugar. Stir in all the remaining ingredients, except the cherries. Mix well together.

2. Place 40 teaspoonfuls of the mixture on to lightly buttered baking trays. Keep the mounds well apart as they spread. Top each with a cherry quarter.

3. Bake until they are a warm gold colour, allowing about 10 to 12 minutes in an oven preheated to 400°F/200°C, Gas Mark 6. Cool slightly.

4. Remove to a cooling rack. Store in an airtight tin when cold.

DANISH OPTIMIST 'CAKES' (Makes 20)

A lovely name for these crunchy, delicate-tasting biscuits topped with almonds.

3 oz (75 g) Danish butter,
  softened
Pinch of salt
4 oz (125 g) plain flour
1 oz (25 g) icing sugar, sifted

Topping
10 almonds, blanched and halved

1. Work all the main ingredients together in a bowl to form a paste.

2. Place 20 small mounds of the mixture on to lightly buttered baking trays. Keep the mounds well apart as they spread.

3. Stud the top of each mound with half an almond.

4. Bake until lightly browned in an oven preheated to 400°F/200°C, Gas Mark 6. Allow about 10 minutes.

5. Cool on a wire rack. Store in an airtight tin when cold

DANISH RUM RINGS

(Makes 30)

These crispy rings can be grouped together in fours and tied on to the Christmas tree.

4 oz (125 g) Danish butter, softened
6 oz (175 g) plain flour, sifted
1½ oz (40 g) icing sugar, sifted
1 egg yolk
1½ tablespoons dark rum

Topping
1 egg white
1½ oz (40 g) walnuts, finely chopped
1½ oz (40 g) granulated sugar

1. Place all the main ingredients in a bowl. Knead together with the fingertips to form a dough.

2. Wrap the dough in foil or cling film. Refrigerate for 30 minutes. Roll out thinly on a floured surface.

3. Cut into rounds with a 3-inch (7.5-cm) cutter. Remove the centres with a 1-inch (2.5-cm) cutter. Re-roll and re-cut the trimmings to make 30 rings.

4. Transfer to buttered trays. Brush with lightly whisked egg white. Sprinkle with nuts and sugar.

5. Bake until golden brown, allowing about 10 minutes in an oven preheated to 400°F/200°C, Gas Mark 6.

6. Cool on a wire rack. Store in an airtight tin when cold.

MOCHA SHORTIES

(Makes 16)

These are crisp, rich biscuits that need careful handling. Do not attempt to make them on a hot day.

6 oz (175 g) plain flour
1 oz (25 g) cocoa powder
3 level teaspoons instant coffee
 powder
2 oz (50 g) icing sugar
6 oz (175 g) butter, softened but
 not runny

1. Sift the flour, cocoa, coffee powder and sugar into a bowl.

2. Cream the butter until light. Using a fork, stir in the sifted ingredients.

3. Draw the mixture together and wrap it in foil or cling film. Refrigerate for 2 hours or until firm.

4. Turn on to a floured surface. Roll into a 'sausage', 3 inches (7.5 cm) in diameter. Cut into 16 rounds with a floured knife. Transfer to ungreased baking trays.

5. Bake until the biscuits are a light gold colour, allowing about 20 minutes in an oven preheated to 325°F/160°C, Gas Mark 3.

6. Remove to a wire rack and leave until completely cold before storing in an airtight tin.

Orange Shorties

(Makes 16)

Follow the recipe above, omitting the coffee and adding 2 level teaspoons finely grated orange peel to the sifted dry ingredients.

BRANDY SNAPS

(Makes 16)

These are delicious, either on their own or filled with whipped cream. Allow plenty of time because Brandy Snaps do require patience and attention.

2 oz (50 g) butter or margarine
2 oz (50 g) soft brown sugar (dark variety)
2½ oz (65 g) golden syrup
2 oz (50 g) plain flour
1 level teaspoon ground ginger
2 teaspoons lemon juice

1. Place the butter or margarine, sugar and syrup in a saucepan. Stand over a low heat until the fat and syrup have melted.

2. Sift together the flour and ginger. Add to the melted ingredients along with the lemon juice. Stir well.

3. Place only 4 teaspoonfuls of the mixture on to a large, greased baking tray, leaving plenty of room between each for spreading.

4. Bake for 8 minutes in an oven preheated to 325°F/160°C, Gas Mark 3. Remove the Snaps from the oven and leave for no more than 30 seconds to firm up slightly.

5. Lift up each one with a flat knife. Roll quickly and loosely round the buttered handle of a wooden spoon. Leave until firm. Slide off on to a wire rack.

6. Use up all the mixture in the same way, to make about 16 Brandy Snaps. Should the unrolled Snaps cool down too much and become brittle, return them to the oven to soften for a minute or two. Store in an airtight tin when cold.

SHREWSBURY EASTERTIDE 'CAKES' (Makes 24)

These Eastertide 'cakes' were mentioned in the Ingoldsby Legends. This recipe comes to you by courtesy of Dutch Wheelbarrow butter.

8 oz (225 g) plain flour
Pinch of salt
¼ level teaspoon powdered
   allspice
4 oz (125 g) Wheelbarrow butter
4 oz (125 g) light Muscovado
   sugar
1 level teaspoon caraway seeds
1 Grade 3 (standard) egg
½ teaspoon vanilla essence
1½ tablespoons cream sherry

1. Sift the flour, salt and allspice into a bowl. Rub in the butter until finely blended.

2. Add the sugar and caraway seeds.

3. Beat the egg thoroughly with the vanilla essence and sherry. Add to the ingredients in the bowl.

4. Using a fork, mix to a soft dough. Wrap in foil or cling film. Refrigerate for 45 minutes.

5. Form into 24 small balls. Arrange on 3 baking trays lined with Bakewell non-stick parchment paper.

6. Press flat with the base of a tumbler dipped in flour, then prick with a fork.

7. Bake until light brown, allowing 15 to 20 minutes in an oven preheated to 350°F/180°C, Gas Mark 4.

8. Cool on a wire rack. Store in an airtight tin when cold.

SEDGEMOOR EASTER 'CAKES' (Makes 24)

A speciality of South West England, this recipe is by courtesy of Dutch Wheelbarrow butter.

8 oz (225 g) plain flour
1 level teaspoon mixed spice
¼ level teaspoon salt
4 oz (125 g) Wheelbarrow butter
4 oz (125 g) light Muscovado sugar
2 oz (50 g) currants
1 Grade 3 (standard) egg
2 tablespoons brandy

1. Sift the flour, spice and salt into a bowl. Rub in the butter until finely blended.

2. Add the sugar and currants.

3. Beat the egg and brandy well together. Using a fork, stir into the rubbed-in mixture to form a fairly stiff dough.

4. Wrap the dough in foil or cling film and refrigerate for about 30 minutes.

5. Roll out thinly and cut into 24 rounds with a 2-inch (5-cm) biscuit cutter.

6. Arrange on greased trays. Bake until lightly browned in an oven preheated to 350°F/180°C, Gas Mark 4.

7. Transfer to a wire rack. Store in an airtight tin when cold.

REFRIGERATOR BISCUITS (Makes 40)

I gave an explanation of how these biscuits work in the recipe for Danish Brown Cakes (page 81). This version is basic and fairly plain, but other variations follow should you wish to ring the changes.

8 oz (225 g) plain flour
1 level teaspoon baking powder
4 oz (125 g) butter or margarine
6 oz (175 g) caster sugar
1 teaspoon vanilla essence
1 Grade 3 (standard) egg, beaten
A few teaspoons cold milk, if necessary

1. Sift the flour and baking powder into a bowl. Rub in the butter or margarine until finely blended. Add the sugar.

2. Mix to a fairly stiff dough with essence, egg and milk, if necessary.

3. Knead the dough until smooth. Shape into a long 'sausage', 2 inches (5 cm) in diameter. Wrap in foil or cling film and twist the ends to seal. Refrigerate for up to 1 week.

4. To bake, unwrap the roll and cut off as many biscuits as you want to bake—or use the full quantity. Make sure the slices are fairly thin.

5. Place the slices on a greased tray or trays, allowing room between each for spreading. Bake the biscuits until they are a light gold, allowing 10 to 12 minutes in an oven preheated to 375°F/190°C, Gas Mark 5.

6. Cool on a wire rack. Store in an airtight tin when cold.

Chocolate Speckle Biscuits (Makes 40)

Make as basic recipe, adding 2 oz (50 g) grated plain chocolate with the sugar.

Orange Walnut Biscuits (Makes 40)

Make as basic recipe, adding 2 oz (50 g) very finely chopped walnuts and 2 level teaspoons finely grated orange peel with the sugar. Omit the vanilla essence.

Lemon Coconut Biscuits (Makes 40)

Make as basic recipe, adding 2 oz (50 g) desiccated coconut and 2 level teaspoons finely grated lemon peel with the sugar. Omit the vanilla essence.

Spicy Cherry Biscuits (Makes 40)

Make as basic recipe, sifting 2 level teaspoons mixed spice with the flour. Add 2 oz (50 g) very finely chopped glacé cherries with the sugar. Omit the vanilla essence.

ACKNOWLEDGEMENTS

Cadbury Typhoo
Danish Food Centre
Dutch Dairy Bureau
Dutch Wheelbarrow Butter
Edward Billington (Sugar)
Egg Marketing Board
Elsenham Preserves
English Country Life Butter
Flour Advisory Bureau
Gale's Honey
Garraways Jams
McDougalls Flour
Progress Bakeware
Snappies Paper Products

INDEX

95